Shenandoah Heritage

The Story of the People Before the Park

by Carolyn and Jack Reeder

The Potomac Appalachian Trail Club
1718 N Street, N.W.
Washington, D.C. 20036

Copyright© 1978 Carolyn and Jack Reeder
All Rights Reserved

ISBN 0-915-746-10-7
Library of Congress: 78-61240

Cover Photo: **Mountain Woman, from the files of L. Ferdinand Zerkel.**

Shenandoah Heritage

What is left in Shenandoah National Park to remind us of the people who lived in its mountains half a century ago?

Exhibits in the Visitors Centers, trails to old farmsites in the Dickey Ridge area, and evening programs at the campgrounds give the tourist an idea of the Park's recent human history. Faint traces of old roads, a crumbling chimney, or a family cemetery deep in the forest make the hiker aware of those who once lived here. A night or two spent in the isolation of a restored mountain cabin—heated by a woodstove, lighted by kerosene lantern, lacking running water—provides a hint of the mountain lifestyle for a few. Even travelers who never leave their automobiles will see the names of mountain families on signs at overlooks above the once-inhabited hollows.

But who *were* the people whose presence lingers here? What were they like? How did they live? The facts and anecdotes in **Shenandoah Heritage** preserve the substance and flavor of their way of life.

Acknowledgements

We want to thank the many people who helped us with this book:

Douglas Zerkel, who started us on the project with the loan of his father's files;

Frank Carvel, Gloria Dean, Ila Gibson, E.H. Huffman, Roy L. Sexton, Aubrey Sisk, Jesse Weakley, and others who talked with us and gave us a feeling for the way things were (the quotations in *Shenandoah Heritage* are from our conversations);

Potomac Appalachian Trail Club members of the 1920s and '30s who recorded their observations and experiences in issues of the PATC *Bulletin;*

Dennis Carter and Milly Heatwole, who gave us access to materials in Park files;

Paula Strain, who paved the way for us to publish;

and our good friend Len Wheat, who gave us literary advice and encouragement throughout the preparation of the manuscript.

PATC Archives.

Shenandoah Heritage:
The Story of the People Before the Park

Page

Part I: The Mountain Way of Life 9
    Breaking the Stereotypes
    Mountain Homes and Life Styles
    Families
    The Delon Taylor Family
    "They Are Kindly and Helpful"
    Transportation and Roads
    Community Life
    Corbin Hollow
    Boyhood in Weakley Hollow
    Health
    Education
    Religion
    Income and Occupations
    Apples, Cabbages, and the Time of Day
    Tools
    Farming
    One-Upmanship
    Moonshining
    "Mr. Frank's" Encounter
    Lawlessness
    The Chestnut and the Mountain Economy
    Technology Changes the Mountain Way of Life

Park II: The Coming of the Park 55
    The Park Movement
    Outsiders Aid the Mountain People
    The Rescue
    From Farmland to Parkland
    Land Owners, Tenants, and Squatters
    Easing the Transition
    Limbo
    Aubrey Sisk
    Where Are they Today?

PATC Archives.

Part I

The Mountain Way of Life

Breaking the Stereotypes

Half a century ago more than 450 families lived in the area we know as Shenandoah National Park. Much has been written about these mountain people. They have been caricatured as hillbillies. They have been stereotyped as unfriendly and shiftless. Many accounts have publicized the squalid living conditions of a few families but neglected to describe the less sensational lives of those who coped with the hardships of their environment. Both sides of the story must be told:
- Some mountain families lived in miserable shacks; others had neat, comfortable homes.
- Some lacked all but the barest necessities; others had small luxuries such as decorative glassware, perfume, and jewelry.
- Some areas such as Free State Hollow were known for being outside the law; others such as Dark Hollow and Dean Mountain had the reputation of being law abiding.
- Some mountain people were illiterate and virtually unaware of the outside world; others read the local papers and wrote articulate letters-to-the-editor.

The variation in socioeconomic level and lifestyle that existed among the mountain people of fifty years ago was probably the same as you would find in any area the same size today.

Mountain Homes and Life Styles

Mountain homes ranged in size from one room to as many as nine. (*See Table 1.*) They varied in style from painted two-story buildings with columned porches through modest frame structures to log cabins. The most luxurious home we know of in the mountain area was a large brick house with fireplaces in nearly every room. The humblest was a one-room, dirt-floored, windowless cabin.

The typical mountain home, however, had three or four rooms and a loft where the children slept. It was a simple frame house or a log cabin chinked with mud, and it had a porch in front. The roofing material was either shakes or tin. Inside, it was furnished modestly, though there was probably at least one piece of old maple or walnut furniture of good quality.

A picket fence hewn from chestnut surrounded the yard, and washtub planters of flowers stood near the house. Outbuildings included a barn or other animal shelter and possibly a smoke house. There was a vegetable dugout for food storage and often a spring house to cool perishables.

The utilities were simple. Kerosene ("coal oil") lanterns provided light. A spring or stream was the source of water. Fireplaces or wood stoves furnished heat, sometimes supplemented by a kerosene heater.

A family often would live in the same house for generations. Sometimes an extra room or lean-to would be added, or perhaps the original building would be covered with weatherboarding. Otherwise, the typical mountain home of the early 1930s differed little from those of a century before.

TABLE 1

Number of Rooms in Mountain Families' Homes

Rooms in Home	Number of Families
1	18
2	71
3	118
4	107
5	67
6	44
7	16
8	10
9	4

Source: Shenandoah National Park Evacuation and Subsistence Homesteads Survey.   *Date:* 1934

Some homes in the Blue Ridge area that became Shenandoah National Park were large, attractive, and prosperous looking . . . .

(located in Warren County, in the northern section of the Park.)

(located on the Spotswood Trail, the present US 33.)

(located in Simmons Gap, in the Park's southern section.)

In some mountain areas the houses were crude shacks . . . .

(located in the Hollow south of the present Rose River Fireroad.)

Most dwellings, however, fell between these extremes. . . .

(located just inside the southern boundary of the Park in Augusta County.)

(located in Richards Hollow in the central section of the Park.)

(located in Madison County.)

(located in Madison County.)

(located in Page County.)

Just as their homes changed little in a hundred years, the standard of living and way of life of some of the mountain people of the 1920s and '30s were typical of the early nineteenth century pioneer settlers. Faced with much the same conditions that had been endured by their ancestors, their energies were necessarily directed toward survival rather than gracious living. They seemed out of place in the twentieth century, a curiosity from another era. So their ways were deemed "backward" or "outdated" even though the environment they were responding to had changed little since the days when such a life style was the norm.

Rugged terrain, poor roads, and lack of transportation were interwoven factors that isolated these mountain people from the outside world. Their restricted experiences and social contacts reinforced differences in speech and customs. In their own unchanging environment these mountain people lived from day to day, from season to season. Being "out of the mainstream of American life" made little difference to them.

Other mountain people, however, were very much in the mainstream of rural American life. Some of these were prosperous farmers whose land was fertile and fairly level. Some were families who lived along the highways that crossed the mountains or in the hamlets on the fringes of the mountain region. These mountain people were adequately educated and kept up with events in the world outside the mountains. Their way of life was indistinguishable from that of most other farm families in the first third of this century.

Families

Historically, the first generation of a mountain family was established when a couple moved into the Blue Ridge, possibly as land owners, perhaps as tenants of a valley farmer, maybe simply settling on unclaimed land. As their family grew, these early settlers cleared and planted more of the land around the cabin.

Years passed, and one by one the children grew up and married. The daughters left home and became a part of their husbands' families. The sons each received a section of the family land, part of it cleared, the rest forest.

The married sons helped their father and younger brothers farm the homeplace, and they all worked together on the new farms. The youngest son and his bride "stayed with Pa" and helped the old folks. They would someday inherit the homeplace.

The grown brothers continued to help each other with clearing and tilling. but as their own sons grew old enough to help out, there was less need for the brothers to work together. Again, father and sons farmed the family land.

When those sons were grown, often there was not enough land to be divided among all. It was this third generation that either left the mountains to find land or hired out to work on a neighboring farm. Again, the youngest son usually stayed on the farm with his parents and eventually inherited the land.

* * *

And so it went. By the 1930s the people in the Park area had deep roots. Their families had lived in the mountains for generations, and their way of life had changed very little. The environment still provided raw materials to meet most of their needs. Wood for homes and barns, for fences, for furniture, and for fuel was readily available. Stone for foundations and walls littered the ground. Fruit, nuts, berries, and "salat greens" abounded. The woods and streams provided small game and fish; ample grass and forage fed their livestock. But it took the efforts of all family members to make daily life run smoothly.

The division of labor in the mountain family was typical of that in other rural areas of the time. The husband farmed, cut wood, constructed and repaired buildings, fences, and tools. He carried grain to the mill and hauled provisions from the general store.

In the mountain family, woman's work truly was never done. She

> *"You got 'due bills' at the store when you traded nuts and berries. They were just as good as money. You couldn't spend 'em anywhere else, but then there wasn't anywhere else to spend 'em."*

had no labor-saving devices. Her household "appliances" were the wood-burning stove, the dishpan, the washtub, the spring house, the broom. The garden was her responsibility also, and she had to "put up" food for winter.

As in all farm families, the children were expected to do their share of work. Both boys and girls helped in the gardens or fields, took care of livestock, and carried countless pails of water from the spring or stream. Older children looked after the younger ones, and all ages gathered nuts and berries to sell.

In the mountain culture, children were considered grown up as soon as they were physically mature. When the boys grew to be as big and strong as their father, they became more his companions than his charges. Then the chores they had done as young boys fell to their already heavily burdened mothers and sisters, and their strong hands lightened their father's work.

The girls learned a woman's role by working with their mothers, and they often married young. They were "bashful and shy but ready for marriage at fifteen." Usually they would marry a youth from a neighboring farm. Throughout the mountain area there was a vast network of families linked by marriage ties.

TABLE 2
Size of Households

Number of People	Number of Households
one person	22
2-4 people	210
5-8 people	173
9-11 people	50
12-14 people	8

(There was an average of five people per family, only slightly above the state average of 4.33 for white families of native parentage.)

Source: Shenandoah National Park Evacuation and Subsistance Homestead Survey. *Date:* 1934

Four sisters: family ties remained strong throughout life.

A young Corbin Hollow family.

Madison County mother and child.

Four members of a three-generation family pose outside their Madison County home. While households varied in size from a single person to 14 members, the average was five people per family. *(See Table 2.)*

The Delon Taylor Family

Delon Taylor and his family lived in Hawksbill Gap, just east of Skyline Drive. As a young man, Delon had moved to that site from Kite Hollow, a few miles to the southwest.

The Taylor house was a two-story structure with a board-and-batten exterior. It had a large front porch and was surrounded by lilacs and a variety of other shrubs, ornamental trees, and flowers. The land around the house was fairly level, and the soil was fertile. There was a large garden and plenty of grass for the horse and cows.

Delon and his wife Hester had a large family—six girls and two boys. Delon was a strict father. He demanded respect and obedience from his children and required them to do many chores. He did not allow them to slip off to meet their friends. In the evenings he taught his sons and daughters to read and write by the light of the kerosene lamps, then sent them to bed at nine o'clock.

The Taylors did the laundry for the nearby Skyland resort. They had large cast iron cauldrons set up near the spring. The family members worked together, filling the cauldrons with boiling water, adding soap and linens, stirring the wash with a wooden paddle, then rinsing the linens in the second cauldron.

Delon and Hester pause from their laundry work.

Lent by Ila Gibson.

The Taylor grandchildren and other relatives enjoyed Sunday get-togethers at the Hawksbill Gap farm.

When his farm was condemned for parkland, Delon had mixed feelings. On the one hand, he wanted to move away because he didn't like his family to be exposed to the outsiders who came into the new Park with their noise and city ways. And he feared that a campground above his home would pollute his spring. On the other hand, he was reluctant to abandon his home and the plants he had nurtured so many years. He sometimes wished that he could be allowed to fence off a small area and live out his life in his familiar surroundings.

When the Taylors had to leave Hawksbill Gap, they did not leave the mountain area Delon loved. They moved just outside the Park boundary to the foot of Stony Man Mountain. Delon and Hester lived there for the rest of their lives, again surrounding their home with flowering plants and enjoying the visits of their grandchildren.

"They Are Kindly and Helpful"

Mozelle Cowden worked with the mountain families, gathering information to use in planning their relocation when the Park was established. Miss Cowden described them as "just ordinary people" who differed little from other Americans. To give an idea of what they were like, she wrote of some of her experiences in the Blue Ridge.

Recently my car was stuck in mud and rocks about fifteen miles from the nearest garage. It was my first visit to the neighborhood. The car refused to move backward or forward. I had no idea where to go for help.

A man walking up the road proved to be the son of a family I wanted to visit. He told me I had passed one house I needed to visit just a short distance back, that if I'd visit it before I went on further I need not come back through the mud, but could go on up the mountain to the Skyline Drive.

After we tried again to get the car out and failed, I asked him what one did in such circumstances. Instantly he said, "Well, what I thought was, a man down the road three quarters of a mile has a team. I can slip down and get it while you see that family. That way you won't lose so much time."

So he "slipped back" and got a team while I made my visit and that way I lost practically no time at all. It took all the combined efforts of the team and engine to get the car out of that mud and up the next red clay hill. Neither the man who had first helped me nor the one who brought the team would make any charge for the service. When I argued that they had helped me and I'd like to give them something, they said I wouldn't have been on that road except to help them, that they were sorry the road was so bad and if I ever had trouble again would I please send for them. They wouldn't take any money.

Several times I've met a problem too big for me to handle without assistance and never has one of our mountain people turned away without offering to help and making the offer good. . . .

Frequently a house is very inaccessible and directions for finding it cannot be clear. It is not unusual for someone to say, "Some of us will walk along and show you—it's pretty hard to find the way if you don't know the paths. We don't mind."

Once the Welfare Supervisor of Park Families and I got lost. We had received directions from the home where we left our car. Just before dark the mother sent her boys out to blow whistles and call along the ridges and she stayed in the yard and "hollered" so we'd know which way to come.

It was the boy with the whistle who led us back up the right path. He spoke as if he had met us accidently and walked on. The mother told us she had been worried and had sent the boys out. When we thanked her she said, "Oh, that's all right—some of us ought to have showed you the way."

Transportation and Roads

Walking was the most common means of transportation in the mountains. It was not unusual for a family to walk from the area east of Skyland to Luray and then return the same day carrying heavy loads of provisions. Men who worked as seasonal farm-hands in the valley typically walked as much as eight miles to reach their jobs. And many Skyland employees lived five miles or more from the resort.

Only about a third of the families in the Park area owned horses, and few had cars or trucks. Vehicles were of little use in most areas because roads were generally primitive; sometimes a home or community was linked to the outside world by only a foot trail.

In the 1920s only three major roads crossed the Blue Ridge in the Park area: the present U.S. Routes 211 and 33, and the Gordonsville Pike at Fishers Gap. Other than these well-used transmountain routes, there were few public roads in the mountains. This situation has been

A mountain man returns from the mill and general store in the valley.

cited as an example of the county governments' reluctance to provide services for people who paid little or nothing into the tax coffers. One critic pointed out that although Madison County appropriated $7,000 for a road over Chapmans Mountain to President Hoover's camp on the Rapidan River, it had no funds to blast the rocks out of the road between Syria and Old Rag.

A variety of nonpublic roads crisscrossed the area, however. Some of these were "private" in that they crossed a farmer's land or led from his farm to another road or to town. Most of these began as animal trails before the area was settled, became the footpaths of the early inhabitants, and were eventually widened for use by wagons. (Road widening operations consisted of dragging a log behind a wagon to clear away rocks and debris. The rocks that collected in front of the log were piled along the roadsides.)

All were welcome to use these private roads, but the accepted code required users to help maintain them. If a large rock rolled down the hillside onto the road, it was up to the traveler to remove it; if a tree fell across the road, the traveler had to cut his way through. And, of course, users had to close gates at property lines to keep livestock from straying.

Other nonpublic roads through the mountains were cut by commercial interests. Some were built by timbering companies to haul out cordwood or tanbark. George Pollock had the Skyland road constructed to provide access to his resort. The road through Browns Gap was built privately in the early 1800s and was operated for profit as a toll road for many years. While some of these roads were passable by automobile, they were not paved, and bad weather made them treacherous.

In fact, it was common for wagons to mire down even on the Gordonsville Pike. The tradition there was that if a driver's team could not free his wagon, he had to give his horses' string of bells as a trophy to the man whose team was able to pull the rig out of the mud.

The lack of good roads in the mountains restricted more than transportation and commerce. It restricted the opportunities and experiences of the people. The social and economic conditions in most communities were directly related to their distance from decent roads.

Community Life

Mountain communities grew up along streams where the land was most fertile. Usually these hollows were known by the name of the predominant family: Keyser, Jenkins, Corbin, Nicholson, Weakley, Hensley....

Other communities were strung along the roads that crossed the mountains at Simmons Gap, Browns Gap, Fishers Gap, and the more heavily traveled Swift Run and Thornton Gaps. The people living in these gaps benefited economically and socially from the transmountain traffic. They were more prosperous and better informed than the families in the isolated hollows.

Although mountain settlements were neither large enough nor geographically close enough to have much organized community life, there was much informal visiting. Distance between homes was no barrier to socializing after evening chores were done. Families often made trips of several miles on foot by lantern light. And as in other parts of the country, relatives met for Sunday dinner and an afternoon of companionship. The children had to play outside or sit quietly in a corner and "listen to their elders." No noise was allowed in the house.

Much of the social life in the mountains accompanied the cooperative efforts of neighbors. Corn huskings were much enjoyed occasions: finding a red ear was rewarded by a drink of brandy. "Some fellows caught on to bringin' their own red ear in their pocket and pullin' it out. They'd get drunk and just fall over on the shucks!" And everyone pitched in at house raisings, apple butter making time, butchering, and "corn hoein's" when a man was too sick to tend his crops.

As in other isolated areas, neighbors were drawn together out of necessity. The community was the only resource for assistance or entertainment.

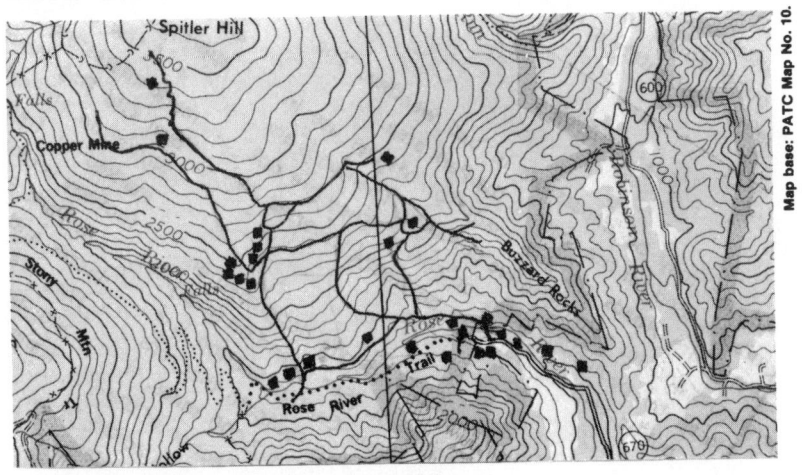

Cluster of homes in Richards Hollow.

Corbin Hollow

The communities that received the most publicity were the ones near Skyland, and the best known of these was Corbin Hollow.

The first Corbin to settle in the hollow that bears the family name was a veteran of the War of 1812. Another family had settled in the area before the Revolution. Descendants of the original Corbin and the pre-Revolutionary War arrival were among those who lived in the hollow in the first third of this century.

During the late '20s and early '30s, the Corbin Hollow families included some believed to be the most impoverished in the Blue Ridge area. George Pollock described them as "emaciated, illiterate, and scarcely able to speak understandable English." It was the abysmally low standard of living of some of the families in Corbin Hollow that brought public attention to the people living in what was to become Shenandoah National Park.

Writers and journalists descended on the area. While they did not claim to write of the Virginia mountain people in general, their readers often assumed that the accounts were representative of people throughout the Park area. This was not the case, nor were all of the people of Corbin Hollow destitute.

A journal entry written after a visit to Corbin Hollow in 1926 and later published in the Potomac Appalachian Trail Club *Bulletin,* is one of the few to give both sides of the picture:

> The first cabin had been built by a subscription raised by the guests at Skyland, for their former cabin had been so wretched. Here were living a grandfather, three sons, and a boy nineteen years old about four feet high. There were three sisters; those who had married had married their first cousins of the same name. There were from ten to twelve children, all bare-foot and barely covered with ragged clothing. The beds were planks built out from the wall, covered with a mess of rags. On a steel bed which had come when the cabin was built, there was one quilt, worn through in half a dozen places, showing the rusty springs. The place was beyond description. The grandfather was not so bad, but each generation had grown worse.
>
> The next place was a shack ten feet square. Here lived a man, wife, and four children. . . . But next was one of the other extreme. This man had a large cornfield, potatoes, cabbage, several pigs, cattle, and lived a life ideal in its vigorous comfort.

Corbin Hollow was the "Colvin Hollow" of Mandel and Sherman's *Hollow Folk* (1933), a sociological study of communities at different levels of cultural development. The authors stated: "No one in the Hollow Proper can read or write. There are no cattle or poultry in the Hollow Proper. One family owns a pig and another a horse." The key word here seems to be Hollow *Proper*. Data collected throughout the entire hollow by Miriam Sizer indicates that while twenty-eight of the adults were illiterate, twenty-nine could read and write some but had skills below fifth-grade level; two had better than fifth-grade skills.

In the entire hollow, there were nine cows, five calves, and 330 chickens. Besides the pig and horse in the "Hollow Proper" there were six additional pigs and a mule.

Nine of the thirteen families in the hollow were judged by Sizer to live in poor or very poor conditions, conditions of overcrowding and filth. She wrote of bathing children in May who had not been washed since the previous September. But to balance the record she also noted that one Corbin Hollow woman was among the few in the entire area surveyed who followed scrupulously sanitary methods of dishwashing.

Corbin Hollow's pocket of poverty was unique in the Blue Ridge. It was no more representative of the standard of living in the Park area than a slum is representative of a city.

> *"There were 'good' hollows and 'bad' hollows, just as there are similar sections in a city. Many folks have taken their concepts from what they have heard of the 'bad' hollows; the more sensational ones."*
>
> —Alvin E. Peterson, PATC *Bulletin*

Boyhood in Weakley Hollow

Jesse Weakley enjoys telling of his boyhood in Weakley Hollow before the land was bought for the Park—the five-mile walk to the Dark Hollow School where he went through third grade . . . his late afternoon chore of "hollerin' after the cows" if they didn't come at milking time . . . 'coon hunting all across Old Rag Mountain . . . catching trout in White Oak Canyon.

"We'd put a hoop in the mouth of a sack, and bend the bottom of the hoop so it would rest flat on the bottom. Then we'd hold that in the river between the rocks where the water was swift while the others would splash and drive the fish downstream. We'd catch twenty-five or thirty trout at a time that way!"

The winters of Jesse's youth were cold, snowy ones. He recalls one year when the snow was even with the top rail of the fences, the year of a wild sled ride down Old Rag.

"Nine of us took a yellow poplar board 'bout six foot long and nailed a seat on the back and a foot rest in front. We came down that hill like a bullet and went right through a big fodder shock at the bottom!"

Another boyhood thrill was swinging on a grapevine from a clifftop forty or fifty feet above the rocky ground.

"Sometimes the vine'd give way, but you'd go down easy 'cause it would be tangled 'round the tree branches. Then sometimes we'd climb up a sapling and hang onto the top while somebody cut it part way through—we'd ride it to the ground."

One experience he remembers vividly was going with his friends to clean out a den of rattlers.

"We shot 179 snakes with our .22s that day," he marvels.

Jesse moved away from Weakley Hollow in 1928, but he has not forgotten the years he spent in the shadow of Old Rag Mountain.

Today, Jesse Weakley lives near Hood, Virginia, in Madison County.

Health

The mountain people were generally hardy folk. If they survived early childhood, they usually lived well into their seventies or eighties. Considering that there was little understanding of germs and in some cases sanitation was minimal, their health was surprisingly good. (*See Table 3.*) Some authorities attribute this to the nutrients in the large amount of cabbage and unrefined cornmeal in the average family's diet.

TABLE 3
Physical Conditions of Park Families *

	Father	Mother	Children
Good	304 (73%)	283 (67%)	1226 (87%)
Fair	74 (17%)	92 (22%)	144 (9%)
Poor	40 (10%)	50 (11%)	63 (4%)

Source: Shenandoah National Park Evacuation and Subsistence Homesteads Survey. *Date:* 1934

Some of the children suffered from infected tonsils and several areas had cases of dysentary in the summer, but the most prevalent health problems were dental. Few people kept their teeth into old age, and most adults' smiles showed gaps left by missing teeth. A 1932 survey of 257 Park residents found that 68 percent had defective teeth, 42 percent had gingivitis—inflamed gums—and 9 percent had pyorrhea—inflammation of the sockets of the teeth. Dental care was virtually unknown.

A mountain man who complained of his bad teeth was asked by the social worker why he didn't have them fixed.

"If you had to choose between having your teeth fixed or feeding your family, which would you choose?"

"Why, feeding my family, of course," she replied.

"Well then, we ain't so different, only you've had money enough for both and I've never had quite enough for the first."

---

*These ratings were made as part of a survey of the Park population by twenty-five Enumerators chosen from among the respected citizens of the eight counties in which the mountain people lived. While the ratings are based on the Enumerators' impressions rather than on scientific data, it is significant to know how the people were seen by their contemporaries.

Many families also lacked money for medical care. Others lived in such remote areas that house calls were impractical and a trip to the doctor was a major undertaking. Then, too, the people were often fatalistic, believing that when your time came you would die and if it wasn't your time yet, you would recover.

Although doctors occasionally visited patients in the Blue Ridge, home remedies or patent medicines were the usual treatment for ailments. Turpentine swabbed on with a feather eased a sore throat, as did a gargle with bloodroot tea. Wintergreen tea soothed arthritic pains. Boneset tea reduced fever. A poultice of cornmeal and onions alleviated chest congestion. It was not until plans were being made to relocate the mountain people outside the newly established Park that medical care came to much of this area of the Blue Ridge.

"Puttin' on Airs"

"Dan was the first person in his community to build a 'johnny house,' and his neighbors made great sport of this pretentious idea. They lined up in his yard to watch him come out to use it. Dan would go along with this and swagger over to his new privy.

"But there was one problem. Dan didn't know you had to dig a pit under the privy, and before long there was a terrific odor. His neighbors, who squatted behind a rock or tree, had no odor problems because of the refreshing rains.

"Poor Dan was a laughing stock for some time after that!"

Education

Educational attainment in the Blue Ridge ranged from complete illiteracy to full literacy. In many cases, the determining factor was location: people living along major roads and near the foot of the mountain region were better educated than those in remote hollows or high on the mountainsides. Age, too, was a factor: the older generation was better educated than the younger since educational opportunities had declined rather than improved as time went on.

A 1932 survey of 132 of the Park families found that 37 percent of the people over six years old were illiterate, 49 percent could read and write with below fifth grade level skill, and 13 percent could read and write above fifth grade level.

Most of the mountain people were disturbed by the lack of educational opportunity for their children. One Dark Hollow resident, regarded as "an able and influential leader among the mountain people in his section," wrote an article for the local papers describing the lack of educational facilities for Dark Hollow children.

The county had opened a public school near Red Gate, now known as Fishers Gap, in the 1870s to serve the Dark Hollow community. The Red Gate School was abolished about 1900. There was no schooling available from that time until around 1918 or '20 when the Dark Hollow Church was built and occasional school terms were held there. When the Hoover School was established several miles to the southeast in 1930, no more education was provided in Dark Hollow. Few children, however, made the difficult trip to the new school.

The people of Hazel Hollow also were concerned about the lack of schooling for the twenty area children. They asked Miriam Sizer, the social worker who aided the mountain people, to help them get a public school in 1932.

One Hazel Hollow man originally had opposed a school in his area, scorning "lowlander learning," as unnecessary for mountain people. An incident involving his son changed his mind. The youth had worked picking apples in Berryville and had earned $12.00 which was paid by check. He had never seen a check before, but the paymaster explained that he could go to a place where he was known and exchange it for money.

The youth took his check to the general store where the family traded. There the storekeeper and another man, deciding to have some fun at the lad's expense, told him that he needed two witnesses to his "X" and must split the check with the witnesses.

When his son returned home with this story, the father began to see the relevance of education for mountain children and joined his neighbors in their appeal for a school.

But not all mountain areas were without education. The Episcopal missions provided schools as well as churches. At least one community—Dean Mountain—built its own school and hired a teacher. And some areas had public schools.

A public school was built in the Old Rag region in 1871 and operated nearly continuously thereafter. By the 1920s the term was nine months long. The school in Richards Hollow actually predated public education in Madison county; it was converted to a public school in 1871. By 1924 Richards Hollow had a two-teacher school and by 1930 the term was eight months long.

It was a different story in the more remote hollows, however. Between 1879 and 1903, Nicholson Hollow had sixteen terms of about four months each; in the next fifteen years there were only two terms totaling four months. As for Corbin Hollow, by 1930 there had been a grand total of nine months of schooling in the settlement's history. And the Crescent Rock community never had a school.

The situation in Page County was typical. Page County included the western side of the Blue Ridge from north of Matthews Arm to south of Lewis Mountain, but only two public schools were located in the Park area in that wide expanse of land. Both of them were in the Thornton Gap area. It is easy to understand that the county would provide its schools in the more densely populated, easily accessible areas. Nonetheless, only thirty-five of the estimated 240 mountain children in Page County were attending school in 1934.

The lack of sufficient educational facilities in the mountain area had far-reaching effects on the people. According to Virginia law, an illiterate person who had less than $250 of taxable property could not vote. And more than half of the families owned no property at all. Lacking the right to vote, the mountain people lacked the political clout to obtain the improved roads and schools that would have helped them better their living conditions.

The Nicholson Hollow schoolhouse was a typical log cabin. Some of the children from Corbin Hollow attended this school.

These children made up the student body of a mission school in Greene County.

Religion

Three levels of organized religion existed in the mountain area, all typical of those in rural areas of the day.

The most formal were the Episcopal mission churches where services were preached by ordained ministers. Next were the community churches. Dark Hollow, for example, had its own church building and minister. Geurdon A. Cave and his sons built a church across the road from their home, and Mr. Cave preached there weekly without pay. The Dean Mountain citizens also built their own church. They supported their minister with gifts of farm produce.

The most loosely structured religious observances were in the communities that had services intermittently whenever a preacher was available. Usually the service was held in the school building. During warm weather a temporary shelter built of brush sometimes provided a place for people to gather to hear the circuit preacher.

Religious services were traditionally Protestant. Apart from the Episcopal mission churches, the main denominations were Baptist, Methodist, and United Brethren. The labels were different, but often there was little else to distinguish one group from another. Sometimes the main factor in deciding which to choose was the personality of the preacher.

"In the mountains, the real religion was survival and the moral code followed naturally."

The Episcopal Church established a home mission in the Pocosin area in 1904 in hopes that religion and education would have a positive influence on the local people's way of life. (A county official quoted in a Potomac Appalachian Trail Club *Bulletin* described the hollow as "more like the floor of Hell than anything else.")

Another Episcopal mission was established in Simmons Gap. Note the bell tower on the right. One of the original mission buildings is now used as the Simmons Gap ranger residence.

A "Brush Tabernacle" was constructed as a shelter for services held when the circuit preacher came. This one, photographed around 1920, was on the mountain between Skyland and Big Meadows.

Making baskets from white oak was a family craft in some hollows.

Income and Occupations

More than half of the mountain families had cash incomes of less than $100 a year in the late 1920s and early '30s. *(See Table 4.)* Very few people in the Blue Ridge had occupations in terms of full-time paying jobs. Usually women kept house and worked the garden while the men farmed. To meet their need for cash, most people sold farm or garden produce and worked intermittently for wages. George Pollock's famous resort Skyland was a ready market for eggs, vegetables, moonshine, and cordwood, and it provided jobs for at least fifty men and women in the Stony Man region.

A handful of men had skilled trades such as carpentry or stone masonry. A few offered their services as millers, blacksmiths, sawmill operators, or merchants. Some earned money through the sale of hand-crafted items. The Nicholsons and Corbins sold the baskets they made from white oak, and a number of men supplied handmade tool handles to hardware stores as far away as Warrenton. There was great demand for hand-split shingles, also; lumbermen and builders regarded these as far superior to the mass-produced variety and bought them at $4.00 a thousand in the early '30s.

TABLE 4

Annual Income of 465 Families in the Park Area

Income	Number of Families
not reported	19
no income	33
less than $100	218
$101—$200	88
$201—$500	78
more than $501	29

Source: Shenandoah National Park Subsistence Homesteads Survey. *Date:* 1934

The greatest source of income for the mountain men, however, was hiring out as seasonal laborers. (*See Tables 5 and 6.*) During apple-picking and corn-harvesting time, most men were able to earn enough to buy their families' winter provisions.

With their farm produce—and occasional help from better-off neighbors or the Episcopalian missions established in some areas—the majority of the mountain people were able to meet their basic needs in spite of their low cash income.

TABLE 5

Occupations Represented in Five Mountain Hollows*
(adults over 18 in 132 families)

farmers	148
housekeepers	139
day laborers	135
lumbering	43
trappers	36
stilling	21
hauling, transportation	18
carpenters	13
basket makers	13
orchardists	11

Source: Shenandoah Inspections and Investigations, NPS. *Date:* 1932

*Nicholson, Corbin, Weakley, Richards, and Dark Hollows.

TABLE 6

Sources of Income for 465 Families in the Park Area

Income Source	Number of Families
labor	308
farming	49
no income	30
moonshine	17
woods	8
roads; hauling	5
handicrafts	6
miscellaneous	25
no information given	17

Source: Shenandoah National Park Evacuation and Subsistence Homesteads Survey.   *Date:* 1934

Apples, Cabbages, and the Time of Day

Frank Carvell has lived all his life in the little town of Overall, not far from the Park boundary. As a youth he knew many of the people who lived on Hogback Mountain and in Compton Hollow.

One day young Carvell drove his mother up Hogback to buy some apples. The orchard was on such rocky land that he couldn't drive the team and wagon through, so he had to carry out the apples in gunny sacks holding two bushels each. Not wanting to make an extra trip, Carvell put a sack under each arm, took a sack in each hand, and carried his eight bushels of apples to the wagon all at once. For months afterward the amazed farmer spread the word around: "You'd better watch out for that feller!"

Mrs. Carvell admired the large cabbages growing in the family's garden and decided to buy some. The farmer began to cut the heads. He cut and cut.

"Hold on!" said Carvell, "I only want a dollar's worth."

The farmer kept right on cutting, explaining as he worked, "I'm goin' to make real sure you get your money's worth."

After Carvell loaded his fourteen cabbages into the wagon, he asked the farmer what time it was. The man climbed up on a fence, looked westward over his shoulder, and estimated 4:20.

"And that was pretty accurate," remembers Carvell, "judging from the time we got home."

Tools

The mountain man maintained his self-sufficiency with the aid of hand tools and a few horse-drawn implements.

Some men owned carpenter tools such as froes and drawknives. These versatile implements were necessary for home building. The froe, a knife-like wedge that was held by a short handle and struck by a wooden maul, split shingles or clapboards. The drawknife, a two-handled blade drawn toward the user, tapered the edges of shingles and shaped floorboards to the proper width. Its other uses included fashioning tool handles and spokes for wagon wheels.

The more prosperous farmers—those with horses—owned plows and sometimes wagons. "Slides" were more common than wagons, however, because of their greater practicality on difficult terrain. These land sleds were especially useful for hauling rocks, logs, or harvested crops. Heavy loads could be pulled across uneven ground that would snap a wagon axle or through mud where wagon wheels would mire down. Another adaptation to the rocky terrain was the use of a "drag" instead of a harrow for breaking up clods after plowing. The drag was a wooden platform that was weighted down with rocks and dragged across the field to pulverize the soil.

But the most universally owned tools were hoes, corn knives and mattocks. (*See Table 7.*) Women used hoes to cultivate the garden, and in areas too rocky to plow a farmer was limited to the primitive method of scratching the soil with a hoe to loosen the surface for planting.

The farmer used the corn knife, a tool with a longer handle and a straighter blade than the sickle, for cutting fodder. The mattock was a double-bladed grubbing tool with one end of the head similar to a pick and the other end like a hoe. This was a necessary tool for cutting out heavy vegetation and working rocky ground.

At a time when tractors were in widespread use on America's farms, the mountain man still farmed primarily by hand.

TABLE 7

Tools Owned by Farmers in Five Mountain Hollows*

Horse-drawn Implements

plows	165
slides	45
wagons	12
harrows	3
drags	2

Hand Tools

hoes	474
corn knives	197
mattocks	88
forks	72
shovels	69
blades	60
rakes	56
crowbars	23
carpentering tools	16
spades	8
picks	7
horseshoeing tools	7
scythes	5

Source: Shenandoah Inspections and Investigations, NPS.   *Date:* 1932

*Nicholson, Corbin, Weakley, Richards, and Dark Hollows.

Farming

The majority of the mountain people were subsistence farmers, cultivating less than five acres. They grew enough vegetables to eat in season and store for winter, and they raised a pig or two to butcher in the fall. Most also had a cow and some chickens. (*See Tables 8, 9 and 10.*)

Although corn was the most important grain raised on mountain farms, a few families also raised oats, buckwheat, or rye. They harvested these crops using scythes or cradles, hauled the grain stalks to the barn on slides, and threshed them with a flail made from a hickory pole. (This method of separating chaff from the grain is virtually the same as that described in the Old Testament.)

Without the use of fertilizers or crop rotation, farmland "wore out" in a short time. The custom was to let the field lie fallow for a few years and break new ground for planting. Often the abandoned field would grow up in bluegrass and be used for pasture.

Preparing a cornfield and bringing the crop to harvest was no easy undertaking. First the farmer had to clear the land. Sometimes he chopped the trees down, sometimes he simply killed or "deadened" them by cutting through the bark's cambium layer all around the trunk. This was a time-saving method of allowing the sunlight to reach the ground. The deadened trees could be cut for firewood or fenceposts at a more convenient time.

Next the farmer chopped out the undergrowth and saplings. If the land was rocky, another necessary step was loading the surface rocks onto a slide and hauling them away, a job the children often helped with. Sometimes the farmer built a wall with the rocks cleared from a field; other times he piled them on top of boulders or around deadened trees.

The "newground" was then broken by plowing. Ideally a horse-drawn plow was used, but if no horse was available, one man would guide the plow while two others pulled it. Man-plowing was also necessary on hillsides too steep for horses.

Usually the farmer broke up clods by cross-plowing since most fields were too rocky to harrow. Sometimes he used a "drag" to pulverize the soil. Next he made furrows with a shovel plow, planted the corn by hand, and hoed dirt over the kernels. In very rocky areas with shallow topsoil, the farmer would drop the kernels on the ground and cover them with dirt from a bucket. Sometimes kernels were planted between rocks so they wouldn't wash away and so the collected heat would speed germination.

Twice during the growing season the farmer plowed between the rows while his wife and children cultivated between the plants with hoes. At the time of the second hoeing he usually thinned the rows, allowing only the strongest plants to remain.

At harvest time the farmer cut and shocked the corn, aided by his older children. After the fodder dried, they shucked the corn and hauled the ears to a gristmill on a homemade slide.

The women and children were responsible for the garden. Staple garden crops were potatoes, cabbage, corn, and beans. These were ideal in that they were easily stored for winter use: potatoes and cabbage kept well stored in the vegetable dugout or in trenches layered with straw; cabbage could also be made into kraut; corn and beans could be either dried or canned. The garden plots did not wear out as quickly as the fields, since in making full use of the available space through the growing season vegetable plantings were alternated.

Growing crops required constant toil; raising livestock was easier. Chickens required little care. Pigs ran wild, foraging in the woods until they were rounded up for butchering. (Notches in the pigs' ears indicated who their owners were.) Cows could graze most of the year and needed to be fed and sheltered only in severe weather.

The mountain people needed only salt, coffee, and a few other staples to supplement their homegrown meat and vegetables and the meal ground from their corn.

TABLE 8

Census of Livestock in Five Hollows* (132 Families)

chickens	5416
pigs	288
cows and calves	174
bee gums (hives)	90
horses	41
turkeys	40
ducks	21
mules	10
sheep	10
guineas	6

Source: Shenandoah Inspections and Investigations, NPS. *Date:* 1932

*Nicholson, Corbin, Weakley, Richards, and Dark Hollows.

TABLE 9
Number of Acres Cultivated by Park Families

Acres Cultivated	Number of Families
none	44
less than one	92
1.0-3.9	103
4.0-6.9	113
7.0-10.9	54
11.0-15.9	30
16.0-100.0	26

Source: Shenandoah National Park Evacuation and Subsistence Homesteads Survey. *Date:* 1934

TABLE 10
Crops and Livestock Raised in the Park Area (462 Families)

Crop	Families Raising Crop
potatoes	71%
corn	64%
oats	15%
wheat or buckwheat	6%
rye	5%
apples	5%
hay	3%

Livestock	Families Raising Stock
chickens	81%
cows	80%
hogs	66%
horses	34%

Source: Shenandoah National Park Evacuation and Subsistence Homesteads Survey. *Date:* 1934

One-Upmanship

Two brothers, one hard-working and one a bit of a rascal, lived a short distance apart on the family acreage.

The hard-working brother sold his surplus farm produce. He cooled eggs and milk in the springhouse overnight and took them down the mountain to sell in town the following day. One morning, though, he found the springhouse empty. The next day—empty again.

The angry farmer decided to lie in wait, all night if need be, to catch the thief, who he suspected was his ne'er-do-well brother. Just before dark he took his gun and settled himself against a tree a short distance uphill from the springhouse door. All night long he watched, but the thief did not appear. When daylight came he stiffly left his post, satisfied that he had made his point: he would not submit to being robbed of his livelihood.

A few minutes later his brother dropped down from the tree where he had spent the night watching the watcher and made one last raid on the springhouse.

Moonshining

Making whiskey or brandy was as natural to the mountain man as baking corn bread or "putting up" fruit was to his wife. These were regarded as equally legitimate uses of the crops best suited to the mountain land and climate.

In general, whiskey and brandy were made for local consumption or for sale at Skyland, although during prohibition some areas accessible by car became suppliers for bootleggers. The average family did not raise enough excess corn or fruit to produce liquor in great enough quantities to sell. But if a mountain farmer did have a large surplus of corn or fruit, the easiest and most profitable way to market it was to convert it to liquor.

The historical precedent for this way of marketing corn—and for the opposition to its taxation—dates back to the very beginning of the nation. The late eighteenth century frontiersman had no way of transporting his surplus corn to eastern markets. By distilling the corn into whiskey he could both reduce its volume and raise its value. And in this concentrated liquid form, corn could be taken across the mountain trails on horseback.

Lack of decent roads was as much a problem for the isolated farmer in the Blue Ridge in the first third of this century as it had been for the frontiersman in the 1700s. And the response to the situation was the same: distill the corn.

The twentieth century mountain man's objection to the tax on his product, however, usually took the form of avoidance rather than confrontation. Instead of banding together to oppose the tax on liquor—as the frontiersman did in the Whiskey Rebellion of 1794—individuals set up illicit stills. The Constitutional amendment prohibiting the manufacture and sale of alcoholic beverages in the United States had no effect on the mountain moonshiners. They continued to operate their stills throughout the Park area: at Gravelly Spring, in Hazel Hollow, Nicholson Hollow, Richards Hollow, Pocosin Hollow, Jarmans Gap, and many other secluded spots with a constant water supply.

Author's photo.

Stills were located in secluded spots throughout the Blue Ridge.

"Mr. Frank's" Encounter

One winter weekend in the late 1920s Frank Schairer and his friend Charlie Williams were hiking in the mountains, chatting with the people they met along the way. Both men were active members of the Potomac Appalachian Trail Club which at that time was constructing the Appalachian Trail and side trails through the Blue Ridge. An experience they had on this hike was still a vivid memory nearly four decades later. Schairer recounted the story at the fortieth anniversary celebration of the Potomac Appalachian Trail Club in 1967:

All of a sudden around a sharp bend in the trail came two mountaineers. One was an older man with a white beard, and the other was a younger man carrying a gunny sack in which it was obvious there were four two-quart jars of corn liquor. So we just sat there. And there was an awkward pause. And then the conversation got going as they do in the great circle of the mountains. . . .

You start with the weather . . . And the next thing you talk about is the crops, which are important to the mountain people, for if the crops are bad they might starve. And then the talk was about illness, miseries, as they called it. And about that time everybody was sick, with inadequate food and inadequate housing, and so forth. And then another adequate topic of conversation was this proposed Shenandoah National Park, was that all nonsense or was it going through . . . And we got back to the weather; if it was a good day, it was a good day for a drink; or if it was a bad day, we needed a drink.

And the fellow says, "Do you fellows ever drink?"

And I said, "I don't mind if I do."

And he brought out a two-quart fruit jar.

Charlie is a nice guy, but he doesn't drink. It was the most embarrassing thing in the world. I rushed up to Charlie and grabbed the two-quart fruit jar. I nearly knocked the him down. I swung the fruit jar up, took a good swig, and swung it down again, and I said, "Charlie doesn't drink, but I drink for him." And I took another swig.

So they thought it was so cute that I got Charlie's drink. And then there was an awkward pause. And it suddenly dawned on me that I had a drink in my pack, and I said, "Won't you have a drink of my liquor?"

And I went over to get it out of my pack . . . I pulled out this pint thermos bottle and handed it to the fellow. And he took a drink and he looked very startled. He took another little drink and he handed it back. I put it back in the pack and tied up the pack and we sat down and there was an awkward pause.

Then the old fellow said, "I can tell you where you-all got that liquor."

And I said, "You can?"

And he said, "Yes. That is Hazel Hollow liquor." (And Hazel Hollow was about 30 or 40 miles to the north.)

And I said, "Yes?"
And he said, "I can tell you who made that liquor."
And I said, "Can you?"
And he said, "That is Jack Dodson's liquor. And I can tell you when you got that liquor."
"How can you tell me that? When I got it, it was in a two-quart jar." (But he was right all the time.)
And he looks at me and said, "You must be Mr. Frank."
Here I give a guy a drink of liquor and he tells me my name! And I said, "Would you mind telling me how you do it?"
He said, "Each hollow has its own formula. There is only one make of liquor in Hazel Hollow, and this is Jack's. And Jack has only made three batches this year. The first batch he was terribly thirsty, so he let the batch burn. It couldn't have been that, because it was burned. And having burned the first batch he was terribly cautious, and the second batch was perfect."
(That was the batch I had. In fact, it was so good that word got around and it only lasted three days. So he knew within three days when I bought it.)
"It couldn't have been the third batch, because he stored it. And Jack never sells any of his liquor to anybody outside the mountains but this fellow Frank, and so you must be Mr. Frank."

> *"Solly was a wood trader, but he didn't seem to sell much wood. His wagon load of logs always looked the same. Actually, he had the logs hollowed out to conceal jars of peach brandy from his still in Jewel Hollow."*

Lawlessness

Much of the so-called lawlessness in the mountains involved types of behavior that were an accepted part of the mountain way of life: moonshining, hunting and fishing out of season, drunkenness and fighting. Records of five hollows in Madison County, for instance, showed that two-thirds of the offences brought to court involved liquor or fighting.

One community, though, had such serious problems of housebreaking, fire setting, and vandalism that at least one family member always remained at home to guard the property. This was not typical of the whole mountain region, although some vandalism and petty thievery occurred at times in several areas.

The more isolated mountain regions were to some extent out of reach of the law well into the twentieth century. County enforcement officers ventured into the mountains only when complaints were made, usually in case of serious crimes such as murder.

And murders there were. Most of them were committed under the influence of moonshine and involved family members or neighbors. Personal violence almost always had a motive: rivalry over a woman, suspected infidelity, an argument over a still.

An interesting observation is that several murders, considerable vandalism, and a rash of fire settings occurred during the years immediately following the establishment of the Park. At this time the people were "living on borrowed time," not knowing how long they would be allowed to remain in their homes. A sociologist might explain some of their lawlessness at this time as the result of "social dislocation."

> *"Stealin' off of somebody was at the risk of your life. The sheriff wasn't called, because you handled it yourself. You shot him and they buried him and that was that."*

The Chestnut and The Mountain Economy

Along with the insecurity about the future caused by the coming of the Park, the people faced a crisis in their everyday lives: the aftermath of the chestnut blight.

Before the blight, the chestnut was the backbone of the mountain economy: its nuts, bark, and wood were all marketable.

People gathered bushels of nuts to sell or use for barter at the store. They hauled huge loads of nuts out of the mountains to be shipped by rail to distant markets. The gatherers had some competition for the nuts, though—foraging hogs. "To get the nuts took three people at least. One to coax the pigs away from the tree with corn, one to shake the tree, and one to gather up the nuts."

Chestnut bark contained tannin, which was in demand for curing leather. Before chemical methods came into use, tannin extracted from bark or wood was used exclusively; it continued to be used in processing high-quality leather goods.

Early in the spring the mountain people would fell a tree, split the bark with a "spudder," and peel it off. As much as a cord of bark could be removed from a large tree. Sometimes the people took their loads of bark to tanneries in Sperryville, Browntown, Luray, Elkton, or Waynesboro. Sometimes they stacked it along the roads to be picked up later by tannery wagons.

Chestnut logs were in demand for use as telephone poles or for milling into railroad ties. The straight trunk and resistance to rot made the chestnut ideal for these purposes.

Besides being a free-for-the-harvesting cash crop, the chestnut played an important part in home economy. The wood had qualities that made it useful to the mountain man: it was easy to work with, and it was almost free of knots. Chestnut wood could be bent into wagon wheel rims, split into shingles, worked into tools, or milled into boards with virtually no knot holes.

Every part of the tree played a role in mountain life. The nuts that fattened the razorback hogs also attracted the squirrels that were so

With his mule and donkey this man hauled load after load of chestnut extract wood to the tannery in Luray. (The wood, as well as the bark, was rich in the tannin needed for curing leather.)

tasty in a stew. Limbs were split for long-lasting fence posts and rails. Bales of twigs were put in gullies to keep the land from washing. The new spring growth—known as "honeydew"—was cut and stored for winter cattle feed. The blossoms attracted so many bees that chestnut groves often marked the starting point of expeditions to locate bee trees.

Then came the blight. Brought into the U.S. on ships from Asia in 1904, the chestnut blight reached the Blue Ridge in the '20s. Within a few years it wiped out the American chestnut and with it a major source of livelihood for the mountain people.

Chestnut "skeletons" were a common sight in the Blue Ridge after the blight.

Technology Changes The Mountain Way of Life

In the nineteenth century there were thriving "industrial complexes" at the foot of mountain hollows wherever rushing streams could power a mill wheel. Besides turning the large stones that ground the farmer's grain, the water wheel drove a vertical sawblade that cut boards from logs dragged to the site. Often a tanner plied his trade in the same complex, using water power to run a bark mill that ground the tanbark used for curing his leather. A carding mill to prepare fibers for spinning into yarn or thread was sometimes part of the complex.

The farmer paid the miller with a one-eighth share of the flour or meal. He dragged his own logs to the sawmill and left two-thirds of the boards as payment. The tanner's customers supplied both tanbark and hides, and the craftsman kept half the hides as his pay. The operator of the carding mill took a tenth of the raw wool for his services.

But by the first third of the twentieth century the gristmill was all that remained. The old stationary "up-and-down sawmill" had been made obsolete by the portable rotary saw that could be set up at the timber tract. The tanner's small business had long ago been displaced by large tanneries located along railroads where they could receive huge loads of hides from the West and tan all but their specialty leathers with chemicals received by rail. The carding mill had become extinct when mass production techniques made "store bought" clothing readily available.

This technological progress took its toll on the mountain people. It robbed them of their self-sufficiency. No longer could they meet most of their need by supplying their own raw materials and paying with part of their yield. They were made dependent on "the outside world," a world that was beyond their reach geographically, economically, and socially.

Shenandoah National Park Boundaries.

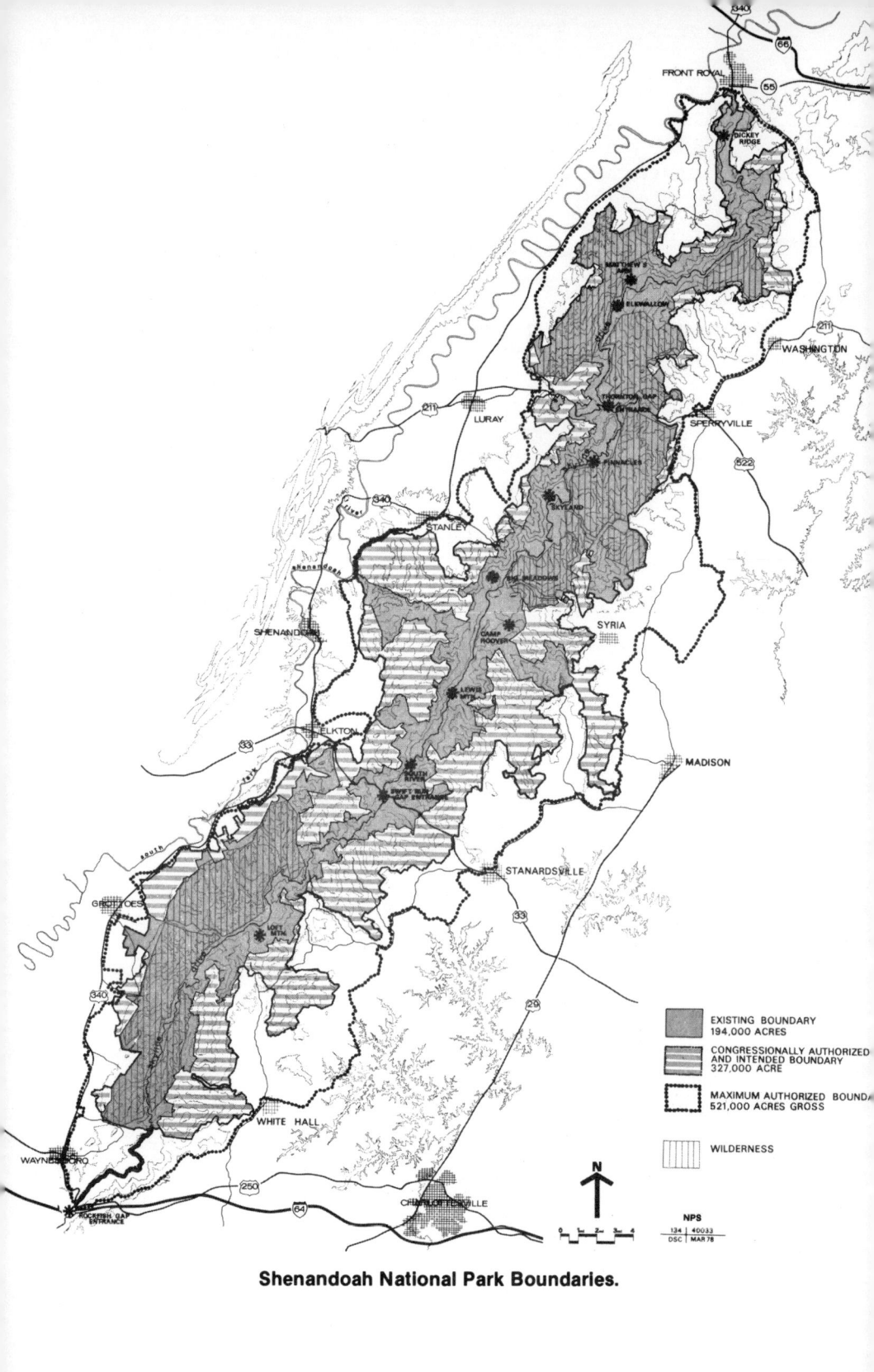

Part II

The Coming of the Park

The Park Movement

As the mountain families went about their daily chores in the hollows and on the slopes, in communities and on isolated homesites, they were unaware of outside events that would alter their lives:

"I should like to see additional national parks started east of the Mississippi. . . . There would be a typical section of the Appalachian Range established as a national park with its native flora and fauna conserved and made accessible to public use," wrote Steven T. Mather, Director of the National Park Service, in his 1923 *Report to the Secretary of the Interior*. These words spurred the movement that resulted in the creation of Shenandoah National Park—and the relocation of the mountain people.

For some time private citizens as well as state and federal leaders had been urging the formation of a national park in the Southern Appalachians. Mather's report added official impetus and resulted in a Joint Resolution of Congress directing Secretary of the Interior Hubert Work to investigate the possibility of establishing such a Park. Early in 1924 Secretary Work responded by appointing the Southern Appalachian National Park Committee. Its role was to choose "the most typically scenic area in the East" for the park.

Harold Allen, a Washingtonian who was a frequent guest at Skyland, clipped a news article announcing the formation of the Committee and its task. He sent it to George Pollock, Skyland's proprietor, with a note: "Why not Skyland?"

Pollock did not respond to the note, and the Committee's secretary told Allen that the group doubted that there was an acceptable park location north of the Smokies. But Allen clung to his belief that Skyland was an ideal park site. Late in the summer of 1924 he took with him to the resort a copy of a questionnaire the Committee provided to those who wished to recommend a park site.

Together Pollock, Allen, and George Judd—another Skyland guest—drafted answers to the questionnaire. As they discussed the advantages of the Blue Ridge location they became more and more excited and convinced that this was indeed potential parkland. Allen returned to Washington and had the draft of the questionnaire typed. He delivered it to the secretary of the Committee just before the deadline.

Meanwhile, a thirteen-county regional organization called Shenandoah Valley, Inc., had filled out a questionnaire recommending the Massanutten Mountain area west of the Blue Ridge as a site for the new park. When Pollock and Allen learned of this, they contacted the secretary of Shenandoah Valley, Inc., and arranged to address the group. They hoped to convince the members that the Skyland area was superior to the Massanutten. Pollock spoke with conviction, and some members of the group agreed to visit Skyland and see for themselves. One of those who made the trip was L. Ferdinand Zerkel. He was won over immediately and became an ardent and influential supporter of the Blue Ridge location.

Zerkel joined Allen, Judd, and Pollock in lobbying for the Blue Ridge site. Pollock invited members of the Southern Appalachian National Park Committee to come to Skyland as his guests, and two of them accepted. Zerkel encouraged the Shenandoah Valley, Inc., members who had not visited Skyland to join the party. The result of this excursion was that (1) the two Committee members enthusiastically decided that their colleagues must visit the area and (2) Shenandoah Valley, Inc., abandoned its support of the Massanutten site in favor of the Blue Ridge.

In order to arouse wider interest in this location, a new organization was formed: the Northern Virginia Park Association. The Association united the three original boosters of the Skyland area, the leaders of Shenandoah Valley, Inc., and a few interested Washingtonians.

The publicity efforts of this group led to support by newspapers in Washington and Richmond as well as nationwide publicity in *National Geographic*. Meanwhile, the three original "Park Nuts," as they called themselves, continued to spend their personal funds to promote their dream.

And in early December of 1924 their efforts were rewarded. The Southern Appalachian National Park Committee recommended "the Blue Ridge of Virginia as the outstanding and logical place for the establishment of the first new national park in the Eastern section of the United States."

In the summer of 1925 still another group was formed to boost the park: the Shenandoah National Park Association. This statewide organization of Virginians lobbied for the passage of the park bill and began raising money to finance the purchase of the land. (The bill specified that "no public moneys" were to be spent.) A successful "Buy an Acre" campaign united citizens throughout the state in working for a common goal. Twenty-four thousand Virginians contributed. The Association's lobbying also brought results: in the spring of 1926 Congress passed the bill authorizing the establishment of Shenandoah National Park.

Some writers have given most of the credit for the Park to the government officials who worked to implement its establishment. But the real founders of Shenandoah were the private citizens who so willingly contributed their time and money to further the park movement.

Each contributor to the "Buy an Acre" campaign received a Donor's Certificate.

Outsiders Aid the Mountain People

As plans to establish Shenandoah National Park progressed, official attention focused on the families that would be displaced. But even before this, outsiders were becoming aware of the mountain people. One reason for this was the popularity of Skyland. Many of the resort's employees were local people, and sometimes nearby residents sold bouquets of wildflowers to the guests. Then too, people from miles around came to watch the entertainment programs arranged by George Pollock. The vacationers, in turn, stopped to visit mountain cabins on their horseback trips.

Beginning in 1928 another group of outsiders came into the Blue Ridge. Their purpose was to build the Appalachian Trail through the area. Members of the newly formed Potomac Appalachian Trail Club (PATC) scouted the region, then built the "*AT*" and side trails. The trail workers got to know the local people, and cabins or fence corners were frequent landmarks in the Club's first hiking guide. References such as ". . . Pass residence of Joe Wood on left . . ." and ". . . pass house on right (Buracker's) with road opposite" were common in the 1931 *Guide to Paths in the Blue Ridge*.

The area and its people received nationwide publicity when President Herbert Hoover bought his mountain retreat on the Rapidan River. Unfortunately, most newspapermen were more interested in a good story than in presenting an accurate account of the local people. Though the reliability of their articles is doubtful, these writers did make other Americans aware of the existence of the Blue Ridge Mountain folk. And as more and more outsiders became aware of the problems facing some of the mountain people, they did what they could to help them.

When Skyland visitors learned of the conditions in the poorer hollows, they began collecting clothing and food for the families who lived there. Physicians who summered at Skyland provided medical care for area children. They gave medicine and vitamins to sickly babies and diphtheria shots to children whose parents would consent. One physician, Dr. Roy L. Sexton, made arrangements for seven Corbin Hollow children to be taken to Washington for tonsillectomies.

The Potomac Appalachian Trail Club established a mutually beneficial relationship with some of the mountain men when the first of the Club's trailside cabins were built. The lumber was cut at the Hazel Hollow sawmill, roof shingles were rived by Jewel Hollow residents, and local men provided the on-site labor.

"Sing for Granny"

"I remember that the Trail Club was going strong in the fall and winter of 1928-29. . . .

"The Mt. Marshall camping trip turned out to be a good-will trip, cementing Club friendship with the mountain people. On their work trip in this section the men had met with friendly cooperation from the men on the mountain. The tact and consideration shown by our boys together with Frank Schairer's charm and enthusiasm won friends everywhere, so when Frank and Andy, Charlie and Ricker were singing around a campfire in the Smoot meadow one night, they found an audience of mountain folk who cordially invited them to come up to the house and 'sing for Granny.' They complied, were served refreshments, and won the confidence and esteem of these hitherto wary people.

"In October a fairly large group of Club members went down to inspect the newly created Trail section in the region of Mt. Marshall. They found that the mountaineers had set the stage for an evening of song. Four huge logs had been cut and drawn up to a good campfire site, plenty of firewood furnished, and a large number of mountain folk there to enjoy the music. Baskets of apples were provided by the hosts who sat back in the shadows and enjoyed the rousing songs led by Frank. The Trail Club group mixed among the mountain people and a permanent spirit of good fellowship was aroused."

Kathryn A. Fulkerson, PATC *Bulletin*

Hazel Hallow Sawmill.

Skyland Guests visited cabins in the nearby hollows, bringing gifts of food and clothing.

A woman from one of the poorer hollows has chosen items from a bundle of clothing collected by Skyland guests.

PATC trail builder Frank Schairer became a friend of some of the Hazel Hollow people and financed a school for their children. President Hoover established another school near his retreat. Besides teaching children, the Hoover School helped prepare adults for life outside the mountains: parents came in the afternoons to learn to read, write, and handle money.

Concern about the economic future of the mountain people prompted Elizabeth J. Winn to found a crafts school at the community of Old Rag in 1931. It was called The Mountain Neighbors Industrial Center, and its purpose was to teach marketable skills. Miss Winn had three large looms for weaving rugs sent to Luray by train and brought across the mountains on muleback. She taught weaving at Old Rag, and twice each week she went to Corbin Hollow to teach sewing to the girls and woodworking to the boys.

Miss Winn marketed the handcrafted items from Mountain Neighbors in Baltimore. She took orders there for the white oak baskets made by the Nicholson family. She also sent patterns and materials to the women who returned finished items for her to sell for them.

The maxim "Give a man a fish and you feed him for a day; teach him to fish and you feed him for life" proved accurate in the case of the aid given the mountain people. Gifts of food and clothing were often misused: supplies of food intended to help a family through the entire winter were eaten in a few weeks; winter clothing was worn threadbare during summer weather. These donations also tended to create in the recipients further expectations of getting something for nothing. Numerous letters were sent from the hollows near Skyland aggressively requesting packages and listing shoe and clothing sizes. One Washington woman who sent two boxes to Corbin Hollow received more than forty requests from people in the surrounding area.

But most of the people in the Blue Ridge were proud and independent and would not accept handouts. When Frank Schairer tried to share his provisions with his Hazel Hollow friends they would refuse, although they were living on sparse rations due to a poor harvest. The majority of the people were industrious and anxious to better their condition in life. They responded positively to the efforts of outsiders to help them by providing schools or marketing their handicrafts; they proved to be skilled and loyal workmen when they were given jobs.

When the time came to plan for the people to be relocated outside the Park, they became the responsibility of the state and federal governments. But before this, concerned individuals took the initiative and helped the mountain people in whatever ways they could.

The Rescue

Visitors to a remote mountain hollow in 1931 made a discovery that stirred the pity and mobilized the efforts of people over a wide area. In a poverty stricken cabin they found a twenty-month old child who weighed only 12 pounds 6 ounces. This child was described as "misshapen, stunted and emaciated and almost without a spark of vitality... (He) more resembled a starved animal than a human being." When his mother was asked what was wrong with her baby, she replied, "He has the undergrowth."

The story of the rescue of this child is best told through the letters of the people involved. Helen Zerkel, wife of L. Ferdinand Zerkel of Luray, took a great interest in the plight of the poor people in the Blue Ridge. Dr. Roy L. Sexton, a Washington, D.C., physician, had both personal and professional concern for the mountain people. Miriam Sizer worked among the mountain peole and was trusted by them. Sally Robinson* was the baby's mother. Her letters were written for her by a variety of people in Nethers Mill and Old Rag, nearby communities with postal service. The letters are reproduced with the original spelling and lack of punctuation.

Dear Sally,

If you remember I am one of the ladies who visited you last May with Dr. Sexton and others.

You told me then that you wanted me to come back and bring the Baby to Luray and a Doctor if it didn't get better but Dr. S. sent medicine and food to it and they told me it was better.

When I saw your husband at Nethers Mill he told me the Baby is sick again.

Now if you will let Dr. S. have the Baby this winter and can bring it to Nethers Mill, I will meet you there and bring it to Luray to a nurse who takes care of Babies and Dr. Sexton (who knows you) will send the medicine and food as he did last year and in the Spring, about May, I *will bring* the Baby *back* to you so fat you won't know it.

You must ask Hal about this and if he wants us to take care of your Baby for just three months and try to make it strong—write me and tell me when to come to Nethers Mill. I will try to meet you there. I promise the Baby will be taken *good* care of and treated *good* and made well if it is possible.

Did you get the warm coat and dress we sent you and the baby things, too?

Please write or phone me from Skyland so I will know that you got this letter.

(from the files of Helen Zerkel)

---

*Names of the family members have been changed to preserve their privacy.

The Robinson home, with its covering of "mountain shingles." (Mrs. Zerkel is at right.)

From the files of L. Ferdinand Zerkel.

January 13, 1931

Dear Helen,

    Dr. Sexton asked me to write you that he has just had a letter from Miss Sizer about the baby that is to go to the hospital. He wants to know if you have gotten the baby or if you have made arrangements for its care.

    We have written Miss Sizer that she is to get in touch with you and have told her that there is at present seventeen dollars for its care and that we can guarantee from twenty-five to thirty dollars a month for its support. Dr. Sexton will appreciate it if you will let him know when you want the money and where you wish it sent . . .

Devotedly,
June

Rhoadesville, Va.
Jan. 14, 1931

My dear Mrs. Zerkel,

    Today Dr. Sexton wrote me stating that he has now seventeen dollars for the care of Hal Robinson's baby at the Luray hospital and that he can guarantee from twenty-five to thirty dollars a month for its maintenance. He wished to know if you have made arrangements for the baby to go to the hospital and wants to know to whom to send the money and when.

If you wish, you could communicate with Dr. Sexton directly. In order to get the child, someone Hal and Sally knows would have to go to the cabin for the child. I would suggest that you write Hal Robinson at Old Rag, telling him you can care for the baby and setting a time for the child to be gotten. Also I would suggest that Hal go with the person who gets the baby as far as Skyland. This would satisfy the mother.

Also, it would be unwise to give them any idea of the money that will be spent for the baby, because they would then want to keep the baby and have the funds sent to them.

I will be only too glad to be of any assistance possible in this work of love. Write me what you decide to do, and I will write Hal advising him to let the baby go.

Sincerely,
Miriam M. Sizer

(The following letter was written on stationery from Jenkin's store.)

Jan 17/31

Mrs. l f Zerkel. Dear Mrs Zerkel;
Your Letter just recd and will have The Baby at Jenkins store on the 24 at 2 oclock hope the weather will be good on that date.

Yours Truly
Mrs. Sally Robinson
Nethers, va

The Robinson Baby, three days after entering the hospital at Luray.

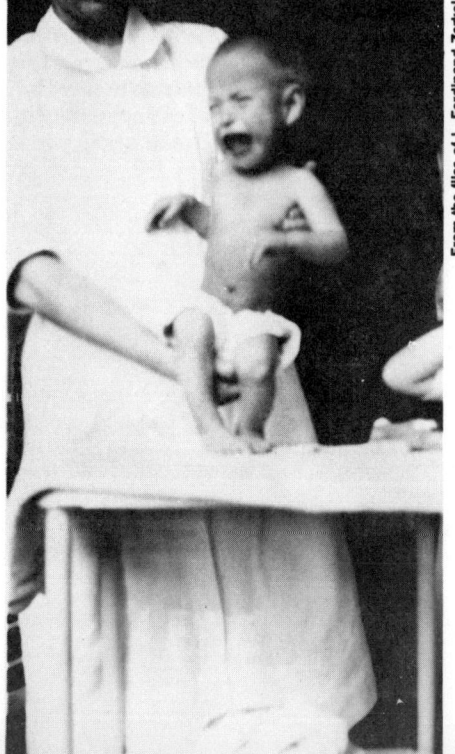

From the files of L. Ferdinand Zerkel.

January the 30, 1931
dear Mrs zerkel

I believed your letter and was glad to hear from you and to hear that the Baby was getting along well I am very thankful to you for Being so kind to us and taking so much intrest in the Baby I trust the lord will reword you for your kindness I know the lord is with all who trust him I would like to see the Baby I miss him so much when you right me again please send the Babys picture in the letter I would be so glad to see you from Sally Robinson

1150 North Capital St.
Washington, D.C.
Feb. 18, 1931

The Page County Memorial Hospital
Luray, Va.
Attention of Mrs. Helen Zerkel

    I am enclosing check for ten dollars a gift from Joseph H. Milaus Chapter No. 41 Order Eastern Star to be applied on the expenses of the Robinson child that Dr. Sexton is interested in.

Sincerely,
(Miss) Rowena F. Roberts

Dear Mrs. L F Zerkel

    I am writing to you to hear from my baby for it has been one month since I herd write and tell me how he is getting a long and you and your family write at once and let me here from my baby for I miss him so hope he is getting better we are all well except colds it is so far to walk to come to see him if you will meat me here at J M Jenkins store I would go up and seen him write and let me know what date you are coming and I will meat you here and if you will bring me back write soon from Sally Robinson

April 14, 1931

Dear Mrs. Zerkel

Just a few linds to let you know how sick I have been the Doctor has been waiting on me I wood like to here abought my baby how he is geting I have not heard from him for five weeks will you please let know abought him and when they air going bring him home let me no soon I wood love to se him from your friend Sally Robinson

* * *

From the files of L. Ferdinand Zerkel.

The Robinson Baby, six months later, in front of the Zerkel family's museum on Luray's Main Street.

After his recovery Sally's baby did not return to his family but was adopted by a childless couple in another part of the state. Within two years after his rescue, his weight was normal and he "possessed a super abundance of robust health, energy, and mental quickness." Miriam Sizer, the social worker, predicted that the child would be "a normal and valued citizen."

Apparently her prediction was accurate. In the early 1970s he held a responsible white-collar position in one of the counties near the mountains he left as a sickly child.

From Farmland to Parkland

Shenandoah National Park was unique: rather than setting aside wilderness for public use, it reclaimed inhabited land. Several thousand people owned land within the boundary originally proposed for the Park. Hundreds more lived on land they did not own but which their families had farmed for generations.

After Congress passed the bill to create Shenandoah National Park, the plan was for the Commonwealth of Virginia to condemn and purchase the land and present the entire acreage to the federal government.

The prospect of the forced sale caused great concern to some landowners. Appeals were made to officials to spare this or that piece of valuable land, to allow a family to retain its small plot, to redraw a boundary to exclude a community from the proposed Park area.

Some of the correspondence speaks eloquently of the conflicts that accompanied the preparations for obtaining privately owned land for the Park. The writers of the letters below are Lee Long, a valley farmer; H. M. Cliser, a home owner in the Thornton Gap area; Arno B. Cammerer, Acting Director of the Park Service; and William E. Carson, Chairman of the Virginia State Commission on Conservation and Development.

* * *

December 15, 1928

Hon. Arno B. Cammerer,
National Park Service,
Department of Interior,
Washington, D.C.

Dear Sir:

In a recent interview with Hon. W.E. Carson, of Front Royal, Va., I was informed that you were the proper person to whom this letter should be addressed.

I am the owner of eleven hundred acres situated on top of the Blue Ridge, lying within the Counties of Madison and Page. The lands have been in the Long family in the neighborhood of sixty years and are regarded as the best grazing lands in the Blue Ridge Mountains, and were so recognized when granted by Lord Fairfax in 1749. All of the land is cleared except about two hundred acres. The property has been used as a necessary auxiliary to farming lands in the Shenandoah Valley, of which I own in excess of three thousand acres. The farming land produces feed to winter the cattle which are grazed during the spring, summer and early fall on the Blue Ridge tract, and the value of my farming land will be very much affected if an adjunct to one of its essential operations is destroyed. Mr. Carson quite understands the situation. In discussing the matter with him he informed me that you have the power to exclude from the Park area the grazing land. The land also contains very valuable mineral deposits.

I am willing to make all reasonable concessions to promote the park proposition and would even consider donating several hundred acres of the tract in timber and granting reasonable easements of passage over the grazing land, if I am not disturbed in the ownership and enjoyment of the latter. Recently I have donated for a distance of a mile and a half portions of some of the most valuable land in the Shenandoah Valley for the purpose of widening the Valley Pike.

As to myself I am pleased to refer you not only to Mr. Carson, but Governor Byrd, to Messrs. Weaver & Armstrong, at Front Royal, and Messers. George Pollock, V.H. Ford and Ferdinand Zerkel, at Luray, Va., in fact to any well known citizen of the Shenandoah Valley. I shall be glad to have you inform me that you will give the matter consideration, and will come to Washington for this purpose if you desire.

Very truly yours,
Lee Long

* * *

UNITED STATES
DEPARTMENT OF THE INTERIOR
NATIONAL PARK SERVICE
WASHINGTON

December 29, 1928

Mr. Lee Long,
Harrisonburg, Virginia

Dear Mr. Long:

I received on the 17th of December your letter of inquiry of December 15 but as there was no address on the letter when it reached my desk I had to inquire of Mr. Zerkel at Luray for it and he has just given it to me.

While there is certain latitude given to us in excluding or including land within the proposed Shenandoah National Park it all depends upon the location. Furthermore, we have authority to lease certain lands after the park has been established, this leasing arrangement to be entered into, however, only after the development of the park as such. I am not acquainted with the location of individual tracts and cannot give you a definite reply until you have furnished me with a map showing the location of the area you own and desire to retain and possibly have made an inspection. Won't you kindly furnish this at your convenience?

Sincerely yours,
Arno B. Cammerer
Acting Director

* * *

Beahm Va
August 17/29

Secretary of Interior
Washington D C

Will the U.S. Government Accept Resident Property from the State of Virginia for the Proposed Shenandoah National Park under Condemnation proceedings under the Condemnation Act I dont feel that I will any thing like recieve for my Humble home what it is worth to me

I will greatly appreciate your reply

Reply H.M. Cliser
Beahm Va

* * *

UNITED STATES
DEPARTMENT OF THE INTERIOR
NATIONAL PARK SERVICE
WASHINGTON

August 19, 1929

Mr. H.M. Cliser
   Beahm, Virginia.

Dear Mr. Cliser:

By reference from the Secretary of the Interior your letter of August 17 has been referred to this service for reply.

The various Federal laws contemplating the establishment of the proposed Shenandoah National Park under certain conditions prescribe only the means by which the park may be accepted when all the land has been acquired by the State. The method of acquisition either by purchase or condemnation is in the hands of the State acting through the Virginia Development and Conservation Commission of which Mr. E.O. Fippen, State Capitol Building at Richmond, is secretary.

Sincerely yours,
Arno B. Cammerer,
Acting Director

* * *

Beahm Va
Sept 3/29

Office Secretary Interior
Washington D.C. Hon Sir

In as much as Some of the democratic Politacal leaders Contributed to the Shenandoah National Park Commisison, Since they see that the Park will undoubtedly be detrimental to the inhabitants of the Area they have used all Possible means and influence to get their lands and their immediate friend lands cut out for instance S.L. Batman a noted democratic leader has succeeded in getting his click run around, J. Gill Grove the Same, W.L. Judd the Same. Please explain why this discrimination is being made.

Reply H.M. Cliser
Beahm Va

* * *

UNITED STATES
DEPARTMENT OF THE INTERIOR
NATIONAL PARK SERVICE
WASHINGTON

September 6, 1929

Mr. H.M. Cliser,
   Beahm, Virginia

Dear Mr. Cliser:

Your letter of September 3rd to the Secretary, calling attention to certain alleged elimination of land from the authorized boundaries for the Shenandoah National Park, has been referred to me for attention since I have been the representative of the Secretary in all matters pertaining to the proposed boundary line for this proposed park.

As you may know, such boundary line as has been officially prescribed, was carefully studied on the ground and is shown on a map, a copy of which I saw posted several days ago in the lobby of the Mansion Inn Hotel at Luray. I am not acquainted with the individual parcels you speak of, but the matter of acquiring the land to correspond with the prescribed boundary line is in the hands of the Virginia Conservation and Development Commission, of which Mr. William Carson of Riverton, Virginia, is the chairman. Doubtless he can inform you regarding the subject matter of your letter.

Sincerely yours,
Arno B. Cammerer,
Acting Director

* * *

UNITED STATES
DEPARTMENT OF THE INTERIOR
NATIONAL PARK SERVICE
WASHINGTON

September 6, 1929

Mr. William E. Carson,
  Riverton, Virginia.

Dear Mr. Carson:

  I am attaching copy of a letter just received from a Mr. H.M. Cliser of Beahm, Virginia, which, together with copy of my reply is self-explanatory. I heard the other day on my trip from Skyland that some large areas were being cut out, thereby modifying the park line considerably as it is laid down on the guide map that was prepared, but I paid no attention to it since I felt it was mere gossip and couldn't be true. The only modification of any extent of which I know is the one which you discussed with me and which lies on Dickey's Hill.

Sincerely yours,
Arno B. Cammerer,
Acting Director

* * *

Riverton, Virginia
September 10, 1929

Mr. Arno B. Cammerer,
Acting Directon,
National Park Service,
Department of the Interior
Washington, D.C.

Dear Mr. Cammerer:

  I waited until today to reply to your letter relative to reports you got as to our cutting out land at different points around the Park area, and also the letter of Mr. Gentry relative to Swift Run till I could have a conference with Mr. Stuart who has direct charge of this work.
  We have been going around the area and have carefully sawtoothed away from your lines* where we could in individual instances satisfy some home holder or small farmer, but we have not been making wholesale cuttings, except at Batman's Cove, and there we have made fairly extensive cuttings, cutting out over thirty homes, two school houses, and four churches.

---

  *In May, 1929, Arno Cammerer and others made an eight-day trip around the Park border, establishing what came to be called the "Cammerer Line" enclosing about 327,000 acres. U.S. Engineers surveyed this line, brush was cleared along its length, and trees were blazed with white paint at intervals. (The Park area was later reduced.)

In the Swift Run section we have had quite a lot of trouble because we would not go up and cut out that village. You will remember it lies on the Spotswood trail between Elkton and Stanardsville; we could not see that it was right to meet these people's wishes, although it would mean the cutting out of at least forty homes. We are carrying out the instructions of Dr. Wilbur, Secretary of the Interior, as correctly as we can and staying as close to your line as is practicable.

As Dr. Wilbur says it would be poor advertisement of the Park to have abandoned farms and homes around the foot of the area. It was his hope that the homes and farms around the Park line should continue in the possession of the people now living there. Added to this we have a hard problem to solve in keeping the people contented, whose land we are taking from them.

It is easy enough to lay down the lines in a whole sale way, but when it is encroaching on thousands of home owners it requires tact, diplomacy, and common sense to keep these land owners from going into frenzy and raising such a howl that the whole Park scheme will be destroyed.

We will be glad to have you go at any time over the lines we have worked out. Then you will see that what we have done has been after careful thought and consideration. I would also like you would (*sic*) discuss this whole matter with Secretary Wilbur and get his reaction.

          Yours truly,
          W.E. Carson

* * *

The village of Swift Run, with its forty or more homes, lay within the proposed Park boundary.

From the files of L. Ferdinand Zerkel.

Page News and Courier
Luray, Virginia
October 25, 1929

MR. CLISER SAYS THE REPUBLICANS ARE AS DEEP IN THE MUD AS THE DEMOCRATS ARE IN THE MIRE

This Park project that is dealing with our constitutional rights in which the high State officials are so much interested, is of a very serious nature, which comparatively few people realize, only because they don't think. You who are so disinterested because it does not concern you, take no part now, but as customs make laws, this may be a stepping stone to interferring with your sacred rights.

The leaders of both political parties have been charged with staining their hands with this attempt and it never has been contradicted.

I listened to a political speech a few days ago by a Republican candidate. He beat all around the bush about equal rights and climbed to the topmost boughs and shook off the leaves of burdensome taxation; then dug up the discrimination in taxation and buried it all on the school house lot there to await the resurrection on the morning after the election. But what seemed to me would have been his strongest point was left out.

While he referred frequently to unjust taxation and the elimination of our rights, he seemed to forget that the homes of the most liberty loving people in the State are threatened. Some one might wonder why this was omitted. Simply because he knew that the garments of the leaders of the Republican party had been dipped and dyed in the same vat.

The fundamental principles of our government are to protect those who can't protect themselves, and to restrain the rich and strong from oppressing the poor and weak, and only eternal damnation awaits any party that gets away from the sound doctrine laid down by our forefathers generations ago. I am a Republican but not the kind that leaves unnoticed or favors a condemnation law that drives widows and orphans or anybody else from home with no where to go and nothing to go with.

As both political parties have been dabbling in this muck as far as equal rights are concerned I see nothing to vote for in the approaching election and the National Park will doubtless be pushed regardless of the result.

The case of the landowners has met with defeat in the circuit court and will, no doubt, in the State court which necessitates our carrying it to the highest tribunal in the land. While this is going to require more money and can't be borne by a few, some may say it's no use to fight the State; we say that States frequently overstep their rights.

A lawyer can be secured at reasonable compensation and on reasonable terms and poor people can't afford to handle their cases separately; as in many cases the estate would be too small for the attorney to consider at all, yet the rich man who is able to litigate with them will get his price for his broad acres and that will make it harder on the owner of small estates, as there will not be enough left to pay them anything, but they will take it just the same.

The little sum it requires, if we all chip in is not at all to be compared with our interests that are at stake. This thing of taking our property away from us is a pretty piece of business. Let's show our officials that we elect them to make laws for us as well as themselves.

Sincerely,
H. M. Cliser.

Beahm, Va., Oct. 22, 1929.

H.M. Cliser tried to save this home by writing to the Secretary of the Interior and by a letter-to-the-editor of the *Page News and Courier* attempting to rally Park area property owners to band together in opposition to the takeover of their homes.

* * *

Despite their efforts, Lee Long lost his mountain grazing lands and H.M. Cliser lost his home. The original acreage proposed for the Park was ultimately reduced by about half; this decision, however, was made on the basis of the high cost of some of the rich farmland, orchards, and timberland rather than on the entreaties of land owners.

Land Owners, Tenants, and Squatters

Once the Park boundaries had been finally determined, every effort was made to ensure that the people who would lose their land received a fair price. A large force of grassland experts, timber technicians, orchard specialists, and building inspectors came into the area to appraise the land, timber, orchards, homes and barns.

More than $1.8 million was spent for Park land. The mountain people, however, received only a tiny fraction of this amount. Most of the mountain land was owned by outsiders. Besides the large tracts of grazing land held by valley farmers, extensive acreage was owned by timber companies and mineral concerns. Over half the mountain people lived on land they did not own. (*See Table 11.*) Some of them were tenants on the land. Some were squatters.

"Squatter" can be a perjorative term, implying shiftlessness or worse. In the Park area, however, there was no correlation between a person's industry or morality and whether he was a land owner. The issue was simply that without equity in the property on which they lived, the squatters—and the tenants—would receive nothing for the land they must leave.

How would those with little or no equity in their homes establish themselves outside the Park? How would those that were poorly educated fare in the outside world? How would those whose work experience was subsistance farming with hand tools find jobs?

With hard work and determination, most of the people coped successfully in their familiar nineteenth century environment, but they lacked both the money and the experience necessary to meet the demands of the twentieth century world outside.

TABLE 11
Amount of Equity of Mountain Families

Amount	Number of Families
None	268
$1.00-$500	61
$501-$1,000	60
$1,001-$2,000	41
more than $2,000	34

Source: Shenandoah National Park Evacuation and Subsistence Homesteads Survey. *Date:* 1934

Easing the Transition

Before accepting the land that Virginia had condemned and purchased, the federal government demanded assurances that the people who were forced to leave their homes would be relocated in areas more suitable for farming and closer to schools, medical facilities, and job opportunities.

L. Ferdinand Zerkel was chosen to take charge of the relocation project. His first step was to survey the Park population and determine its needs. Twenty-five Enumerators canvassed the entire Park area in 1934. They visited the homes of the 465 families still living in the Park area* and completed a comprehensive questionnaire on each one. On the basis of the data collected, Zerkel made plans for resettling the people outside the Park.

Sixty-four families had their own plans and would need no assistance in relocating. A few of the elderly were recommended for special permission to stay in their homes, leasing the land from the Park. Two hundred ninety-three families were chosen as homesteader prospects to participate in a federally funded program to help them build new lives outside the Park. The remainder—many of them older people who might not be able to repay the government loans that would finance the homesteads—were turned over to the state welfare department.

The next step was to locate and purchase enough land for the homesteads. Besides having soil suitable for cultivation, the sites had to be in areas where the local citizens and governments were sympathetic to the program, where there were job opportunities, and where the school systems could handle additional children. Civic leaders, county officials, and potential employers all responded positively to the idea of having relocation settlements in their areas. At last, after extensive field work and correspondence, seven sites were chosen. *(See Table 12.)*

The plan was to provide each family with a homestead including a house, a combination barn and poultry house, a vegetable storage and meat house, and a pig pen with a fenced pig lot. Some families would be provided with full-time farms of 50 or 60 acres. Most would receive 15-acre subsistence farms and would hold outside jobs.

---

*Most of the financially independent families had relocated before the survey was made. This must be remembered when interpreting the charts in this book. The charts are an accurate representation of the so-called typical mountain families, but they do not reflect the whole spectrum of mountain life before the Park was established.

After buying the land, a total of about 6300 acres, Zerkel and his staff coped with the usual difficulties of large-scale building operations plus the frustrations of the political turmoil that surrounded the project, sometimes threatening its completion. It was not until late in the fall of 1937 that the resettlement homes in some of the tracts were finished and the families began to move out of the Park.

> *"People laughed when some of the mountaineers relocated at Ida Valley dragged their bathtub outside and used it to scald hogs in at butchering time. But it was just a matter of values and priorities: they needed something to scald hogs in a lot more than they needed something to bathe in."*

Every effort was made to ease the transition from mountain dweller to "level lander." A Home Demonstration Agent taught the women canning and other homemaking skills; experts from the **Virginia Polytechnic Institute joined County Agents** in training the men in farming methods. The State Department of Public Health agreed to provide free health care for five years.

There was a strong feeling among all those who worked toward the relocation of the mountain people that this would be a great positive force in their lives. Mozelle Cowden, a home economist on Zerkel's staff, wrote.

"We hear so much about the freedom these people are about to lose. They have been free to till soil that is so rocky and steep that most of it must be cultivated by hand. They have been free to live without medical care and without schools; their total gross income wouldn't permit them to call doctors if they were within reach; they do not know dental care, nor can they buy sufficient clothing; their houses are often log huts daubed with mud. They have about the same freedom as birds have to build their nests, get what food they can, to live well in good seasons, and suffer, sometimes die, when the season is unfavorable. They have existed by clearing new patches of land as they wore out what they had and by cutting timber for cross ties and for tan bark. If the forests and land are to be conserved, this practice will have to stop. If the people are to be self-supporting, prosperous citizens, they will have to have better opportunities."

But when a woman who grew up in Dark Hollow was asked about the hardships of life before her family was relocated in Ida Valley, she replied wistfully, "Yes, times was hard, but those was the happiest years of my life."

From the files of L. Ferdinand Zerkel.

These resettlement homes in Ida Valley had running water and electricity. When one woman first saw her new home she exclaimed that it was "the biggest thing I ever seen—and the purtiest!"

TABLE 12
Relocation Sites

Tract No.	Name of Tract	County Location	Total Acres	No. of Families	Farm Economy Full Time	Farm Economy Part Time
1	Ida Valley	Page	365	20	0	20
2	Elkton	Rockingham	1,193	51	3	48
3	C.B.I. School	Greene	575	29	0	28
4	Wolftown	Madison	1,546	54	9	45
5	Madison	Madison	59	20	1	19
6	Washington	Rappahannock	689	27	2	25
7	Flint Hill	Rappahannock	1,464	50	10	40
	TOTAL		6,391	250	25	225

Source: Shenandoah Park Homestead Records. *Date:* 1936

Limbo

More than ten years elapsed between the passage of the bill establishing Shenandoah National Park and the relocation of the mountain people. This transition period was at best unsettling, at worst, traumatic.

Many of the mountain people had refused to believe that they would have to give up their homes. One man, thinking that the Park would allow him to keep his farm, invested in materials for a new roof and an addition to his cabin. The money he received for his property barely covered what he had spent.

A tenant farmer who had been told by the landholder years earlier that he could remain on the land all his life did not realize that the situation had changed beyond the landlord's control. He refused to leave. His family was forcibly evicted, their furniture was moved out, and the house was torn down before their eyes. (Although this was an isolated incident, it received considerable publicity.)

To this day, people in the valley tell about the owner of a fine mountain home who felt that the price offered for his property was too low. He believed that since he had refused to accept the payment offered the land was still his, and he held off government representatives with his gun. But one day the man and his wife had to be away from home. They returned to find that a CCC crew had razed their house. Their belongings had been carried into the yard, true; but little care had been taken with them. The livingroom curtains dangled in a pot that had been simmering on the stove, and the CCC boys were lounging on the mattress, dressed in the couple's clothes.

Some families, however, while apprehensive about leaving the only homes they had ever known, were glad to have the opportunity to relocate near schools and medical care. Also, as time went on, life in the mountains was becoming more and more difficult. In part, this was due to natural causes: drought, extremely hard winters, the chestnut blight. In part it was due to problems created by the establishment of the Park.

Things had changed. The special use permits that allowed the people to stay in their homes allowed little else. The provision that "land not cultivated last year shall remain not cultivated" restricted the practice of letting worn-out fields lie fallow and clearing new ground for crops. The provision that "grazing of cattle will not be allowed in the section of the Park Area between the Lee Highway and the Spotswood Trail" cut out a major source of livelihood for those in the central section of the Park who had been hired to oversee herds for valley farmers. And, of course, no hunting or fishing was allowed, and no living trees could be cut. This kept men from augmenting their families' sometimes meager food supply with small game and from earning money by woodcutting.

Perhaps one of the most difficult aspects of life in the mountains after the establishment of the Park was that the people no longer controlled their own lives. They were now the focus of both state and federal government intervention. Decisions were being made about their future—about where they would live, and how they would live, and when they would leave their mountain homes to begin the new life that had been chosen for them.

An Alternative Viewpoint

"This noon I had lunch with . . . assistant editors of the *National Geographic Mazagine*. They are all interested in parks and we talked and talked about different park matters.

"Two of these men . . . had an interesting point of view on the Shenandoah and Great Smoky Parks. They claim that we ought to leave the old timers in the parks. They say that people don't want to see scenery, that they want to see human habitations and human activities as well. They claim that one of the reasons why so many people go to Europe is that every place one goes there he sees interesting and unique people and structures. They claim that if there was only the scenery of the Alps no one would think of going to Switzerland. They go there because of the unique mountain structures, picturesque people, and the habits and customs of these people. They thought we would make a great mistake if we put all of the mountaineers out of these parks or seriously tried to change their habits of living. . . ."

                        Memo from the Office of the Director,
                                  Department of the Interior
                                            March 25, 1930

From the files of L. Ferdinand Zerkel.

The coming of the Park brought work to some of the mountain men. They helped build Skyline Drive and blast the tunnel through the Great Pass Mountain.

Lent by Ila Gibson.

Several Civilian Conservation Corps camps were established in the Park. Some of the young men in the area joined the CCC, and the $25 a month they sent home helped their families immeasurably.

83

Aubrey Sisk

Aubrey Sisk grew up in the mountains. He spent his youth at his grandparent's farm on Old Haywood Mountain.

Always energetic, Aubrey worked hard around the old folks' place. He hewed chestnut pickets for a fence around the yard. He made two vegetable dugouts for food storage. But his most ambitious project was to build a chimney onto his grandparents' cabin to enclose the stove pipe. The pride he felt in his workmanship was reflected in the stone plaque he carved and set into the chimney: "Built Sept. 1928 by A.H. Sisk."

As was the local custom, Aubrey and his grandfather operated a still not far below the cabin. They sold the whiskey to George Pollock, proprietor of Skyland. One day Aubrey was carrying a burlap sack full of jars of moonshine toward the resort when he came around a curve in the trail and found himself face to face with a revenue man. Turning back he found another officer behind him! Aubrey dashed his sack against a rock to destroy the evidence and escaped by leaping off the rocky ledge beside the path.

Not long after this experience, Aubrey married Delon Taylor's daughter Zula. Aubrey and Zula lived with the Taylors until the coming of the Park forced them to relocate outside the boundary.

When the Park was established, Aubrey did what he could to help the inevitable changes go as smoothly as possible. Since he knew which improvements on the land in his area were legitimate and which had been erected hurriedly in order to bring a better price, he accompanied the land appraisers to help assure that fair values were set. As a leader among the local people, he urged his neighbors to cooperate in the relocation project.

When the CCC was established and camps were set up in the Park area, Aubrey joined the Corps. He helped build the tunnel through the Great Pass Mountain and did much of the stone work and sign work you see along the Drive. The pavillion at Pinnacles Picnic Ground is one of the many structures he helped build.

After the homestead farms were completed by the government-sponsored resettlement project, the Sisks moved to Ida Valley, near the base of Hawksbill Mountain. There the family lived for eight years. Aubrey worked as a carpenter in addition to keeping up with the farm chores and earned enough to pay back the government loan on his homestead.

After he left Ida Valley, Aubrey worked in construction projects in nineteen different states. But Virginia's mountains were his home, and he returned to live in Stanley, within sight of the Blue Ridge.

Young Aubrey Sisk.

Ila Sisk, the firstborn of Aubrey and Zula's five children, sits in the chair her father made for her third birthday present. She was six years old when the family left the Park and relocated in Ida Valley.

Where Are They Today?

After their relocation, the people who had lived in the Park area were exposed to the same influences as other rural Americans and were gradually absorbed into the mainstream of twentieth century life.

But what has become of the mountain people and their decendants? Some have returned to the Park—as rangers, as maintenance men, and as employees at all levels in the Virginia Skyline Company, the Park concessionaire. Some work in the construction trades. Some own thriving farms and orchards; others are ministers, secretaries, school bus drivers, factory workers, homemakers. . . .

There is still misunderstanding and resentment toward the Park: "They said they was givin' us the farms in Ida Valley and then they tried to make us pay. The gov'ment lied to us then same as it does now," and "Yes, they took my people's land and didn't pay'em. And they'd worked that land for years," are frequent comments.

A few of the descendents hunt illegally on ancestral land inside Shenandoah, firmly believing that the land is rightfully theirs. And those who live near the boundary still fear that the Park will be expanded, displacing them once more.

But many former residents have a more positive attitude toward the Park. Some return to the family land to look for "mirkles," the mushroom delicacies that grow in deserted orchards in the spring. Others visit the graves of loved ones buried inside the Park and maintain the cemetery plots. A few take their children or grandchildren on pilgrimages to the family homeplace to give them a sense of their mountain heritage.

Occasionally a former resident will visit the old homesite after years of absence and find a forest where there was once open field or only a pile of rubble where the family hearth once stood.

In gathering information about life in the Blue Ridge before the Park, we visited and talked with a number of former mountain people and their now-grown children. Without exception these people were gracious and cordial. Although we were strangers, they willingly invited us to their homes and shared not only their memories but often treasured family photographs as well.

The people we met were unpretentious. The things they showed us with pride included sparkling rows of home-canned vegetables; pea plants already five inches tall in early April; hand-crafted baskets; and, more than once, a mountain view from the front room window.

And as they pointed out the peaks that had sheltered their homes, their expressions would soften and they'd being to speak of the way it used to be . . . .